Nature Journal

This notebook belongs to
naturalist:

_____

Date: _____

Today's discovery: _____
_____

Time: _____   Location: _____

Description: _____
_____

It was interesting because: _____
_____

My sketch/sample:

Date: _____

I see: _____

_____

I hear: _____

_____

I smell: _____

_____

I feel: _____

_____

Notes: _____

_____

_____

_____

_____

_____

Date: _____

Today's discovery: _____

_____

Time: _____ Location: _____

Description: _____

_____

It was interesting because: _____

_____

My sketch/sample:

Date: _____

I see: _____
_____

I hear: _____
_____

I smell: _____
_____

I feel: _____
_____

Notes: _____
_____
_____
_____
_____

Date:_____

Today's discovery: _____

_____

Time: _____ Location: _____

Description: _____

_____

It was interesting because: _____

_____

My sketch/sample:

Date: _____

I see: _____

_____

I hear: _____

_____

I smell: _____

_____

I feel: _____

_____

Notes: _____

_____

_____

_____

_____

Date: _____

Today's discovery: _____
_____

Time: _____ Location: _____

Description: _____
_____

It was interesting because: _____
_____

My sketch/sample:

Date: _____

I see: _____
_____

I hear: _____
_____

I smell: _____
_____

I feel: _____
_____

Notes: _____
_____
_____
_____
_____
_____

Date: _____

Today's discovery: _____

_____

Time: _____   Location: _____

Description: _____

_____

It was interesting because: _____

_____

My sketch/sample:

Date: _____

I see: _____

_____

I hear: _____

_____

I smell: _____

_____

I feel: _____

_____

Notes: _____

_____

_____

_____

_____

_____

Date: _____

Today's discovery: _____

_____

Time: _____ Location: _____

Description: _____

_____

It was interesting because: _____

_____

My sketch/sample:

Date: _____

I see: _____
_____

I hear: _____
_____

I smell: _____
_____

I feel: _____
_____

Notes: _____
_____
_____
_____
_____
_____

Date: _____

Today's discovery: _____

_____

Time: _____   Location: _____

Description: _____

_____

It was interesting because: _____

_____

My sketch/sample:

Date: _____

I see: _____
_____

I hear: _____
_____

I smell: _____
_____

I feel: _____
_____

Notes: _____
_____
_____
_____
_____
_____

Date: _____

Today's discovery: _____
_____

Time: _____   Location: _____

Description: _____
_____

It was interesting because: _____
_____

My sketch/sample:

Date: _____

I see: _____

_____

I hear: _____

_____

I smell: _____

_____

I feel: _____

_____

Notes: _____

_____

_____

_____

_____

_____

Date: _____

Today's discovery: _____
_____

Time: _____ Location: _____

Description: _____
_____

It was interesting because: _____
_____

My sketch/sample:

Date:_____

I see:_____

_____

I hear:_____

_____

I smell:_____

_____

I feel:_____

_____

Notes:_____

_____

_____

_____

_____

Date: _____

Today's discovery: _____
_____

Time: _____   Location: _____

Description: _____
_____

It was interesting because: _____
_____

My sketch/sample:

Date:_____

I see:_____
_____

I hear:_____
_____

I smell:_____
_____

I feel:_____
_____

Notes:_____
_____
_____
_____
_____
_____

Date: _____

Today's discovery: _____

_____

Time: _____ Location: _____

Description: _____

_____

It was interesting because: _____

_____

My sketch/sample:

Date: _____

I see: _____
_____

I hear: _____
_____

I smell: _____
_____

I feel: _____
_____

Notes: _____
_____
_____
_____
_____
_____

Date: _____

Today's discovery: _____

_____

Time: _____   Location: _____

Description: _____

_____

It was interesting because: _____

_____

My sketch/sample:

Date: _____

I see: _____

_____

I hear: _____

_____

I smell: _____

_____

I feel: _____

_____

Notes: _____

_____

_____

_____

_____

_____

Date: _____

Today's discovery: _____
_____

Time: _____ Location: _____

Description: _____
_____

It was interesting because: _____
_____

My sketch/sample:

Date:_____

I see:_____
_____

I hear:_____
_____

I smell:_____
_____

I feel:_____
_____

Notes:_____
_____
_____
_____
_____

Date:_____

Today's discovery: _____

_____

Time: _____ Location: _____

Description: _____

_____

It was interesting because: _____

_____

My sketch/sample:

Date: _____

I see: _____
_____

I hear: _____
_____

I smell: _____
_____

I feel: _____
_____

Notes: _____
_____
_____
_____
_____

Date: _____

Today's discovery: _____
_____

Time: _____   Location: _____

Description: _____
_____

It was interesting because: _____
_____

My sketch/sample:

Date:_____

I see:_____

_____

I hear:_____

_____

I smell:_____

_____

I feel:_____

_____

Notes:_____

_____

_____

_____

_____

_____

Date:_____

Today's discovery:_____
_____

Time:_____ Location:_____

Description:_____
_____

It was interesting because:_____
_____

My sketch/sample:

Date:_____

I see:_____
_____

I hear:_____
_____

I smell:_____
_____

I feel:_____
_____

Notes:_____
_____
_____
_____
_____
_____

Date: _____

Today's discovery: _____

_____

Time: _____ Location: _____

Description: _____

_____

It was interesting because: _____

_____

My sketch/sample:

Date:_____

I see:_____
_____

I hear:_____
_____

I smell:_____
_____

I feel:_____
_____

Notes:_____
_____
_____
_____
_____

Date:_____

Today's discovery: _____

_____

Time: _____ Location: _____

Description: _____

_____

It was interesting because: _____

_____

My sketch/sample:

Date:_____

I see:_____
_____

I hear:_____
_____

I smell:_____
_____

I feel:_____
_____

Notes:_____
_____
_____
_____
_____
_____

Date: _____

Today's discovery: _____

_____

Time: _____ Location: _____

Description: _____

_____

It was interesting because: _____

_____

My sketch/sample:

Date:_____

I see:_____

_____

I hear:_____

_____

I smell:_____

_____

I feel:_____

_____

Notes:_____

_____

_____

_____

_____

_____

Date:_____

Today's discovery: _____
_____

Time: _____   Location: _____

Description: _____
_____

It was interesting because: _____
_____

My sketch/sample:

Date: _____

I see: _____

_____

I hear: _____

_____

I smell: _____

_____

I feel: _____

_____

Notes: _____

_____

_____

_____

_____

_____

Date: _____

Today's discovery: _____

_____

Time: _____ Location: _____

Description: _____

_____

It was interesting because: _____

_____

My sketch/sample:

Date: _____

I see: _____

_____

I hear: _____

_____

I smell: _____

_____

I feel: _____

_____

Notes: _____

_____

_____

_____

_____

_____

Date:_____

Today's discovery:_____
_____

Time: _____ Location:_____

Description: _____
_____

It was interesting because: _____
_____

My sketch/sample:

Date: _____

I see: _____
_____

I hear: _____
_____

I smell: _____
_____

I feel: _____
_____

Notes: _____
_____
_____
_____
_____
_____

Date: _____

Today's discovery: _____

_____

Time: _____   Location: _____

Description: _____

_____

It was interesting because: _____

_____

My sketch/sample:

Date: _____

I see: _____
_____

I hear: _____
_____

I smell: _____
_____

I feel: _____
_____

Notes: _____
_____
_____
_____
_____

Date:_____

Today's discovery:_____
_____

Time:_____ Location:_____

Description:_____
_____

It was interesting because:_____
_____

My sketch/sample:

Date: _____

I see: _____
_____

I hear: _____
_____

I smell: _____
_____

I feel: _____
_____

Notes: _____
_____
_____
_____
_____

Date: _____

Today's discovery: _____

_____

Time: _____ Location: _____

Description: _____

_____

It was interesting because: _____

_____

My sketch/sample:

Date:_____

I see:_____
_____

I hear:_____
_____

I smell:_____
_____

I feel:_____
_____

Notes:_____
_____
_____
_____
_____
_____

Date: _____

Today's discovery: _____
_____

Time: _____ Location: _____

Description: _____
_____

It was interesting because: _____
_____

My sketch/sample:

Date: _____

I see: _____
_____

I hear: _____
_____

I smell: _____
_____

I feel: _____
_____

Notes: _____
_____
_____
_____
_____
_____

Date: _____

Today's discovery: _____
_____

Time: _____ Location: _____

Description: _____
_____

It was interesting because: _____
_____

My sketch/sample:

Date: _____

I see: _____
_____

I hear: _____
_____

I smell: _____
_____

I feel: _____
_____

Notes: _____
_____
_____
_____
_____
_____

Date: _____

Today's discovery: _____
_____

Time: _____   Location: _____

Description: _____
_____

It was interesting because: _____
_____

My sketch/sample:

Date: _____

I see: _____
_____

I hear: _____
_____

I smell: _____
_____

I feel: _____
_____

Notes: _____
_____
_____
_____
_____
_____

Date: _____

Today's discovery: _____

_____

Time: _____ Location: _____

Description: _____

_____

It was interesting because: _____

_____

My sketch/sample:

Date:_____

I see:_____
_____

I hear:_____
_____

I smell:_____
_____

I feel:_____
_____

Notes:_____
_____
_____
_____
_____
_____

Date:_____

Today's discovery: _____

_____

Time:_____ Location: _____

Description: _____

_____

It was interesting because: _____

_____

My sketch/sample:

Date: _____

I see: _____
_____

I hear: _____
_____

I smell: _____
_____

I feel: _____
_____

Notes: _____
_____
_____
_____
_____
_____

Date: _____

Today's discovery: _____

_____

Time: _____ Location: _____

Description: _____

_____

It was interesting because: _____

_____

My sketch/sample:

Date:_____

I see:_____

_____

I hear:_____

_____

I smell:_____

_____

I feel:_____

_____

Notes:_____

_____

_____

_____

_____

_____

Date: _____

Today's discovery: _____
_____

Time: _____ Location: _____

Description: _____
_____

It was interesting because: _____
_____

My sketch/sample:

Date: _____

I see: _____

_____

I hear: _____

_____

I smell: _____

_____

I feel: _____

_____

Notes: _____

_____

_____

_____

_____

_____

Date: _____

Today's discovery: _____

_____

Time: _____ Location: _____

Description: _____

_____

It was interesting because: _____

_____

My sketch/sample:

Date:_____

I see:_____

_____

I hear:_____

_____

I smell:_____

_____

I feel:_____

_____

Notes:_____

_____

_____

_____

_____

_____

Date: _____

Today's discovery: _____
_____

Time: _____   Location: _____

Description: _____
_____

It was interesting because: _____
_____

My sketch/sample:

Date:_____

I see:_____
_____

I hear:_____
_____

I smell:_____
_____

I feel:_____
_____

Notes:_____
_____
_____
_____
_____

Date: _____

Today's discovery: _____

_____

Time: _____ Location: _____

Description: _____

_____

It was interesting because: _____

_____

My sketch/sample:

Date:_____

I see: _____
_____

I hear: _____
_____

I smell: _____
_____

I feel: _____
_____

Notes: _____
_____
_____
_____
_____

Date:_____

Today's discovery:_____
_____

Time:_____   Location:_____

Description: _____
_____

It was interesting because: _____
_____

My sketch/sample:

Date: _____

I see: _____

_____

I hear: _____

_____

I smell: _____

_____

I feel: _____

_____

Notes: _____

_____

_____

_____

_____

_____

Date: _____

Today's discovery: _____

_____

Time: _____ Location: _____

Description: _____

_____

It was interesting because: _____

_____

My sketch/sample:

Date: _____

I see: _____
_____

I hear: _____
_____

I smell: _____
_____

I feel: _____
_____

Notes: _____

_____

_____

_____

_____

_____

Date:_____

Today's discovery:_____
_____

Time:_____ Location:_____

Description: _____
_____

It was interesting because: _____
_____

My sketch/sample:

Date: _____

I see: _____
_____

I hear: _____
_____

I smell: _____
_____

I feel: _____
_____

Notes: _____
_____
_____
_____
_____

Date: _____

Today's discovery: _____

_____

Time: _____ Location: _____

Description: _____

_____

It was interesting because: _____

_____

My sketch/sample:

Date: _____

I see: _____

_____

I hear: _____

_____

I smell: _____

_____

I feel: _____

_____

Notes: _____

_____

_____

_____

_____

Date: _____

Today's discovery: _____

_____

Time: _____ Location: _____

Description: _____

_____

It was interesting because: _____

_____

My sketch/sample:

Date: _____

I see: _____

_____

I hear: _____

_____

I smell: _____

_____

I feel: _____

_____

Notes: _____

_____

_____

_____

_____

_____

Date:_____

Today's discovery:_____

_____

Time:_____   Location:_____

Description: _____

_____

It was interesting because: _____

_____

My sketch/sample:

Date:_____

I see: _____
_____

I hear: _____
_____

I smell: _____
_____

I feel: _____
_____

Notes: _____
_____
_____
_____
_____
_____

Date:_____

Today's discovery: _____
_____

Time: _____   Location: _____

Description: _____
_____

It was interesting because: _____
_____

My sketch/sample:

Date:_____

I see: _____
_____

I hear: _____
_____

I smell: _____
_____

I feel: _____
_____

Notes: _____
_____
_____
_____
_____
_____

Date: _____

Today's discovery: _____

_____

Time: _____   Location: _____

Description: _____

_____

It was interesting because: _____

_____

My sketch/sample:

Date:_____

I see:_____

_____

I hear:_____

_____

I smell:_____

_____

I feel:_____

_____

Notes:_____

_____

_____

_____

_____

Date: _____

Today's discovery: _____
_____

Time: _____   Location: _____

Description: _____
_____

It was interesting because: _____
_____

My sketch/sample:

Date: _____

I see: _____
_____

I hear: _____
_____

I smell: _____
_____

I feel: _____
_____

Notes: _____
_____
_____
_____
_____
_____

Date: _____

Today's discovery: _____

_____

Time: _____ Location: _____

Description: _____

_____

It was interesting because: _____

_____

My sketch/sample:

Date:_____

I see:_____

_____

I hear:_____

_____

I smell:_____

_____

I feel:_____

_____

Notes:_____

_____

_____

_____

_____

Date: _____

Today's discovery: _____

_____

Time: _____   Location: _____

Description: _____

_____

It was interesting because: _____

_____

My sketch/sample:

Date:_____

I see: _____
_____

I hear: _____
_____

I smell: _____
_____

I feel: _____
_____

Notes: _____
_____
_____
_____
_____
_____

Date: _____

Today's discovery: _____

_____

Time: _____   Location: _____

Description: _____

_____

It was interesting because: _____

_____

My sketch/sample:

Date:_____

I see:_____

_____

I hear:_____

_____

I smell:_____

_____

I feel:_____

_____

Notes:_____

_____

_____

_____

_____

_____

Date:_____

Today's discovery: _____

_____

Time: _____ Location: _____

Description: _____

_____

It was interesting because: _____

_____

My sketch/sample:

Date: _____

I see: _____

_____

I hear: _____

_____

I smell: _____

_____

I feel: _____

_____

Notes: _____

_____

_____

_____

_____

Date:_____

Today's discovery: _____
_____

Time: _____   Location: _____

Description: _____
_____

It was interesting because: _____
_____

My sketch/sample:

Date:_____

I see:_____
_____

I hear:_____
_____

I smell:_____
_____

I feel:_____
_____

Notes:_____
_____
_____
_____
_____

Date:_____

Today's discovery:_____
_____

Time:_____   Location:_____

Description: _____
_____

It was interesting because: _____
_____

My sketch/sample:

Date:_____

I see:_____
_____

I hear:_____
_____

I smell:_____
_____

I feel:_____
_____

Notes:_____
_____
_____
_____
_____

Made in the USA
Coppell, TX
13 March 2020